# Trump: All The King's Men

# **Table of Contents**

# **Introduction**

Donald J. Trump has been the most controversial figure in the 2016 United States elections. His ride down the elevator to announce his run for the Presidency of the United States was received with mixed reviews; most of which included a level of unabashed humor at the thought of a TV host running the most powerful country in the world.

Over the months, it soon became obvious that Donald Trump would change the perception of the USA, no matter the outcome of the election. His blatant, and sometimes completely gobsmacking, stances on national and international policies began to gain serious traction.

This is mainly because his comments made for some really good TV and he aired on channels continuously without being fact-checked. Red began to sweep the state, despite the common rhetoric and polls saying that Trump couldn't make it... Right?

His win was met by a shock that resonated across the world. People couldn't believe he had managed to take on one of the most important positions in the world. Donald Trump would now have a considerable impact on the course of United States' history, as well as the fate of multiple nations on the planet. A presidential run that was tainted with sexual assault allegations, scandals, and many other issues, had managed to beat a long-time politician, Hilary Clinton.

The fall of the presidency in the view of the Democratic Leadership had started even before the election, but it was cemented after the win. Soon, the Presidency began to face serious turmoil as details of the unrelenting Russian scandals began to come out. This, combined with the umpteen mistakes and controversies of the White House, continued to weaken the highest position of the country.

# Chapter 1: The Pre-Election Era

Tracing the Russian scandal back to its roots is not an easy task. The road is paved with a lot of controversies and scandals that involve a huge group of people. It encompasses a lot of different institutions of the country from social media to politicians. However, it is important to understand the problem to its fullest extent to analyze exactly how much damage to the presidency has occurred.

The US intelligence agencies traced the first reports of the targeted hacking to May 2016. The Democratic Party was severely breached by Russian hackers in an attempt to target Hilary's campaign. The role of Wikileaks on the outcome of the 2016 election has been considerable since the hacking led to almost 20,000 internal emails being leaked on Wikileaks, right on the eve of the Democratic National Convention. The contents of the leaks highlighted the party's leadership trying to sabotage the Bernie Sanders campaign. This led to the resignation of

Debbie Wasserman Schultz who has been appointed to chair the DNC.

Attention diverted onto Trump who invited Russian hackers to target his opponent's personal email account at a campaign rally. He suggested, "Russia if you're listening, I hope you're able to find the 30,000 emails that are missing." This statement was so shocking because it was a front-runner Republican politician calling on a foreign power to hack another politician. The absurdity of the situation wasn't lost on the general public and this may have been the first few signs that the Democrats were going to use the word "collusion".

Despite such statements, Trump continued to stand off against USA's intelligence agencies by continuously trying to direct the blame of the hacking away from Russia. He suggested that it could have been China or even an American who conducted the hacking.

More eyebrows were raised when Wikileaks began dumping thousands of Clinton emails an hour after the infamous Hollywood Access Tape was released. The Democrats thought this was too great of a coincidence since the emails were the perfect cover by Donald Trump to hide behind after the infamous tape had been released. While Wikileaks did not reveal their source, Democrates believe that Russia had something to do with these email leaks.

The problem intensified when Paul Manafort's scandal began to unfold. He was accused of taking millions of dollars to boost Russian interests in the United States and Ukraine. Along with Rick Gates, Manafort's dealings with a Russian oligarch led to a more softened position on Ukraine in the Republican Party manifesto. As a campaign manager, Manafort pushed Russian political positions. He was essentially being paid to spread Russian agenda within the country. Eventually, in 2018, he was charged with eight counts of financial fraud, tax evasion crimes, lobbying foreign interests and conspiracy to defraud the US government. However, the damage had been done by that time as Donald Trump was indeed the president.

Paul Manafort wasn't the first person to plead guilty to charges of links with the Russian investigation. George Papadopoulos, the first person to plead guilty, joined Trump's campaign in March

2016 and had ties to Russian officials through an unnamed professor. This professor was also the source through which the Trump team learned of that Russia had thousands of emails of Hilary Clinton. This information was relayed to Donald Trump and colleagues in a meeting inside the Trump Tower. He regularly met with significant officials in the Trump campaign often including Jeff Sessions, Paul Manafort and Rick Gates, as well as foreign officials.

Their dealings with Russia weren't the only thing that led to Donald Trump's eventual win; the man also had the help of his son and son-in-law. Donald Trump Jr. brokered a meeting with Natalia Veselnitskaya, a Russian lawyer, with the help of Rob Goldstone. The emails exchanged to confirm the meetings promised dirt on Hilary Clinton, as well as Don Jr.'s enthusiasm for this information. He and Jared Kushner attended the meeting in Trump Tower, while Donald Trump was in the building.

Don Jr. later suggested that the meeting had just been about a useless Russian adoption policy. However, even agreeing to meet to get dirt on a political rival with foreign powers is not a crime. It didn't matter, however, since Donald Trump acknowledged the meeting had been about political opposition research. Questions about obstruction began to rise when Trump lawyers allegedly let out that Trump had dictated his son's lie about the meeting.

This wasn't the only step they took to accommodate their father's win. His correspondence with Wikileaks showed that they gave him tips on some strategy points to win the election. When it appeared that Trump would lose, they urged him to reject the results of the election, which would have led to a considerable weakening of the democratic process. They also passed along links for him to share. One included a claim that Hilary Clinton actually wanted to fire drones at Assange. Another link they shared was to a website that allowed people to rifle through the hacked emails of John Podesta. Don Jr. did not hesitate to share both of these links, which shows that he intended to win by any means necessary; even if that meant colluding with foreign powers, according to the Democratic Leadership.

Attending the meeting wasn't the only role in the Russian scandal of the son-in-law, Jared Kushner. He continues to be investigated by the FBI for failing to disclose his meetings with Russian

Ambassador, Sergey Kislyak, and Russian banker Sergey Gorkov. Mixed statements by Sergey Gorkov and the Trump administration led to more discrepancies, especially when coupled with the omission of the meetings by Jared Kushner. By May 2017, those meetings have been scrutinized even more as they may have been an attempt to establish a direct link with the Russian president, Vladimir Putin. This is a dangerous sentiment since Jared Kushner received top security clearance and attended several intelligence briefings. If there is any collusion there, this could have been seriously dangerous for the general public, but this was shown to be false, another unfounded claim by Democratic Leadership.

As the election was fast approaching in November, Russian interference stories were already breaking out. Wikileaks of Hilary Clinton's emails, with a little help from the investigation launched by Comey, eventually led to her downfall. Amidst scandals and investigations, Donald J. Trump managed to secure the presidency through the Electoral College.

This led to considerable shock throughout the world. The Democrats thought that Donald Trump was surely unqualified but had run his presidential campaign with a certain flair that won him a considerable base. While his voting base had been large, the investigations and criminal charges on his cabinet members and political supporters in the following months did indeed weigh heavily on his win.

# Chapter 2: The Transition into Trump Era

During the transition period, Trump began to gather his cabinet members and officials. Soon, Trump made the decision to hire Michael Flynn as his National Security Advisor. Flynn resigned in 3 weeks after he failed to disclose his contacts with Russian officials during the election in 2016, as well as in the transition period. On the day when sanctions on Russia were announced by the Obama administration, he also attended several calls from Sergey Kislyak, the Russian ambassador. The calls were meant to soothe the ambassador, as well as agree to push the Russian agenda within the United States. His backing on a Russia nuclear power plant, as well as insistence to Sergey Kislyak to set up direct communication lines with the Russian government, led to him pleading guilty for lying to the FBI in 2017.

A lot of roads lead back to the jolly Sergey Kislyak, the Russian ambassador. He was a well-respected politician who worked hard to push the Russian agenda in the United States, rather effectively. He was involved in the famous meeting at the Trump tower and was one of the main reasons behind the Accusations against Michael Flynn and Jared Kushner. As a high-ranking Russian official, he did nothing wrong by sitting with American officials; however, the problem comes when those individuals failed to disclose meetings with the ambassador. His role may be unclear, but he was the reason behind another problem in the White House.

Jeff Sessions was one of the first politicians to legitimize Trump during the elections by showing him support. He was rewarded for his support for Donald Trump by being appointed as the Attorney General. Upon becoming nominated for the position of attorney general he had to attend some hearings to get confirmed. During the hearings, he confirmed to the public that he had never met with any foreign officials. Despite his written and oral denial of such meetings, there was plenty of evidence that later came out about his meetings with Sergey Kislyak. His failure to disclose meetings with foreign officials led him to face serious backlash.

This was not all. In a statement by George Papadopoulos, it was noted that Jeff Sessions had also attended the meeting where he had informed the Trump campaign about possible dirt on Hilary Clinton via emails. It also raised some serious questions about potential perjury prosecution. If this was true, then Jeff Sessions had also colluded with foreign powers.

Such allegations led to Jeff Sessions' recusal from the Russian Investigation later on in March, much to the indignation of Donald Trump. Trump continues to show rage against the Attorney General for this step, even going so far as to suggest that if he was going to recuse himself then why did he take the position in the first place. The impact of these statements contributed to the chaos inside the White House which shows a broken front instead of a united front the country's president needs to show. This refusal, however, has managed to remove him a bit from the harsh spotlight shone by Robert Mueller. Another person to have barely escaped much of the public's indignation and great scandals was Rex Tillerson. He escaped just in time to avoid going down in history as part of Trump's administration. He was the head for oil and gas companies who dealt often with Russia. He worked for 40 years for ExxonMobile which is one of the largest oil and gas companies in the world.

His appointment as Secretary of State despite close relations with Russians and alleged bias towards oil companies was a surprise to many. He had a lot of contacts in Russia and his objectivity was questioned by many people including Senator McCain. While working for Donald Trump, his lobbying and stance on Russian sanctions hindered the UN's work on the issues with Crimea and Ukraine. He finally left the Trump administration in May of 2018, leaving behind a chaotic White House.

Carter Page and Michael Cohen weren't so lucky as to escape the public's eyes. Carter Page was appointed as the policy advisor for the Trump administration. It was later found that he met with Russian officials in July 2016 and was the main intermediary between Paul Manafort and Russian officials. Michael Cohen, Trump's personal lawyer at the time, also met with

Russian officials in August 2016. He also broke plenty of campaign finance laws, but that is another matter altogether.

# Chapter 3: Under Trump's Presidency

Trump's administration was plagued with different scandals almost every day as soon as it began. The first day in office was met with one of the biggest protests in the history of America. There was no way to know that James Comey would also become a part of one of the biggest controversies to hit the administrations. James Comey first came into attention when he reopened the FBI's investigation into Hilary Clinton a mere few weeks before the election. Democrats speculate that this is the reason behind Clinton's loss. Republicans, including Trump, hailed him as a hero with many praises being sung on the campaign trail.

A few months into Trump's presidency, James Comey was leading the investigation into Trump's ties with Russia. His work into the investigation on Michael Flynn and the president himself made Donald Trump very uneasy. On multiple occasions, Trump tried to befriend him, but when those efforts became futile his Twitter soon became filled with comments against James Comey.

On March 20th, James Comey testified in court confirming an investigation into the Russian meddling in the 2016 elections. In May, in another hearing at the Senate, he declined to talk about the evidence pertaining to the Russian investigation which made Trump very angry. His denial did not help Trump's lawyers in any way and in the Democrat's eyes affirmed that there was indeed evidence against Donald Trump.

He was soon fired by the President and this led to considerable outrage by the Democratic Party and to allegations of obstruction on the president. The White House released that Comey had been fired due to his handling of the inquiry into Clinton's emails, something Trump had previously been ecstatic about. This statement was also rather surprising since the email scandal had been almost half a year prior to the firing of the FBI director. Trump continues to be angry at James Comey for cementing the Russian investigation, and as of August 2018 has unleashed over 50 tweets about him since his firing.

Soon after he was fired from his job as the FBI director, he was called in front of the Senate for a testimony. While under oath he informed the public that Donald Trump had asked for a pledge of loyalty, as well as to "let go" of the investigation into Michael Flynn. Comey also admitted to "leaking" confidential government owned documents to a college friend of his, in the hopes that his friend would leak it to the media and it would spark a special counsel against President Trump. A week later, Robert Mueller was appointed to head the Russian Investigation as a special counsel.

Although Robert Mueller has remained really quiet about the whole operation, many details have continued to come out through other sources. Most of the details, according to the Democratic Party, were leaked by Trump's own lawyers, aides, and associates. Donald Trump raged on every platform of the media about Mueller's probe into all of the President's men. Other details were brought to light when charges were filed against key members of the Trump campaign. Mueller's investigation aimed to look only at Russian meddling turned into an all out free for all. He started to investigate everyone and everything he could to dig up any crimes or unethical behavior by anyone in working for the Trump's Presidency. His investigation branched out in all directions including tax evasion and financial fraud.

His investigation, with an independent budget which has now cost taxpayers a huge sum of over 8 million dollars (and still climbing), led to charges being filed against 32 individuals, as well as many Russian citizens that are not on US soil, so they will never have a chance to be heard. The others include some main Trump's men, some of whom have struck plea deals, including Paul Manafort, Michael Flynn, Michael Cohen, Sam Patten, George Papadopoulos, and Rick Gates. With the leaks and these charges, his work has been a constant hindrance to the Trump presidency and a major waste of taxpayer money and resources. To the Democrat's, as Mueller gets closer and closer to the root of the Russian investigation, the legitimacy of Trump's presidency remains dubious. This weakness is in the Democrat's eyes is further cemented by Trump's public rage over the investigation and Robert Mueller.

His twitter is full of anger fuelled tweets about Robert Mueller, even going as far as to hint a relationship between Mueller and Comey. The relationship has been proved that Mueller was Comey's personal friend and mentor. He has often called for Jeff Sessions to order the end of the Mueller investigation, which raises questions about obstruction in the Democratic Party's eyes. Even if it isn't a crime, it still hurts the Trump case since it seems like a panicked attempt at saving himself. His tweets on James Comey have already allegedly been taken as evidence into obstruction by Robert Mueller.

Despite such a deep investigation and Trump's insistence that "No one has been harder on Russia than me", Trump's ties with Russia have never been better. His continued praise of Vladimir Putin, even going as far as to congratulate him on his 'win' in the 2018 Russian election, has become a recurring issue. The Democrats felt that his refusal to confront Putin on Russian meddling in elections is a weakness. Trump has, however, enforced some of the strongest sanctions against Russia unlike never before. He has also, on many occasions, condemned them for election interference. According to the Democrats, there have been no serious attempts made to protect future elections, except for Facebook's CEO being called in for questioning. This is not true of course. The Trump administration has gone to great lengths to try and stop Foreign Actors from meddling in US Elections. This is a conflict on two opposing sides; one being that the serious doubt that the Democrats feel can weaken American democracy and the credibility of the presidency. This whole belief is just an imaginative thought of the Democratic Party.

The Democrats also felt that when Trump shared sensitive "code word" material with Russian officials and praised Putin on his intelligence for not responding to sanctions drafted by Obama it was a truly problematic. That was just as what is being called today as "Fake News". The true reason behind the lack of response may have been there simply because Russia knew the sanctions would not last. Such underlying nuances from the Obama era only legitimize the power of Russia since it seems like they can play around with American politics without any consequences. This stands to pitch away at American power on the international level in a significant way.

Donald Trump's positive view of Vladimir Putin continues despite the latter's amusement at the

American president. At the press conference in Moscow, Trump was asked whether he believed American intelligence agencies or Putin. He clearly informed the media that he didn't see any reason why it would be Putin, denouncing his own country's intelligence in favor of the dictator. Trump's opinion did not come without cause and justification, as to the use of the intelligence community by Obama to spy on Trump and his associates from the last election.

This statement did baffle many as a minor look at the history of Russia and America's relationship would answer that question immediately.

What was more shocking was Putin's statement just a few seconds later. Putin was asked whether he wanted Trump to win the elections and if he had directed any officials to help him win. He very clearly, and boldly, answered, "Yes, I did" right after watching the American president deny his own country's intelligence for him.

This is not the only instance where he attempted to use the presidency and elections to portray that the United States is weak. In several interviews, he has used the situation of American elections to highlight that democracy as a political system is weak. This idea has been highlighted in Russian media a lot to affirm his power as a dictator and spread the propaganda in Russia against democracy. The Democrats feel he continues to manipulate Trump to cement his own power, which can be seen in the congratulations he received from Trump on his win in the 2018 elections. The reality of that is just ignorant on the Democratic side. They feel Trump's congratulations legitimized the farce elections in Russia where Putin won with an overwhelming majority. The relationship between Russia and America is a true signifier of just how strong the presidency in the United States has become.

# Chapter 4: Effect of the Russian Scandals on the Presidency

The Trump Era started off with a tumultuous beginning. Winning the election for the highest office doesn't automatically mean that you can start wielding significant significance onto the country's institutions. The stigma of Russian meddling, the endless investigation, and charges against significant members of the Trump administration have left a mark on the Trump presidency. Many Democrats believe that he isn't qualified for the job for the presidency and with doubts on how he won; his influence is considerably thin with them. But none the less, he is President as he won the election by electoral vote. The Democrats need to remember that voting machines in all states are not interconnected and the machines were never hacked. There conspiracy theories of hacked elections are just that; a conspiracy theory.

Barely two years into his presidency, he has already lost 35 White House staff through firings and dismissals and 32 more individuals have been charged by Robert Mueller, most of who aren't associated with him. Every day a new scandal hits the White House, leaving the media scrambling and public astounded. With so much going on, it is a wonder that the White House has been able to focus on actual work.

His first few months into the presidency saw challenges in many departments. He was unable to win on health care, despite giving up on his initial agenda of lettings things like Medicaid and pre-existing conditions protections remain. He lost ground on foreign policy with allies trying and failing, to work with Trump. Despite controlling the Senate and the House, the Republicans barely managed to squeeze by with the Tax bill as well. This was due to infighting amongst Republicans and did not relate to the efforts by the President. His challenge for border funding and the immigration deterrent of separating families launched by the Obama administration faced a considerable backlash. The President only followed the Law that was outlined by the Democratic Congress under President Obama. Illegal entry into the Country is a crime. Just as if a citizen was stopped for a crime and had children with them, the citizen would be arrested and children services would be called for the children. But the Democratic rhetoric that no policies were kept in place to reunite them from inept individuals like Chuck Schumer and Nancy Pelosi has had a negative effect on Trump's reputation. His policies on global warming have also faced serious criticism from the national and international community. The criticism is also because America has been the largest "donor" to the Paris Climate Agreement, which is based on GDP and carbon emission amounts. Trump is questioning the legitimacy of the agreement and the actual science behind it really does not make for a good argument. His concerns are real and many feel that this agreement is more of a money-making opportunity than an actual viable entity. Trump was right to question it and to pull out of the accord.

The key issue here is that Trump has to deal with an imaginary Russian investigation and ridiculous scandals that have tried to hinder the ability of the White House to function efficiently. The White House finds itself putting out fires left, right and center. The Democrats that push these ridiculous accusations feel that it will help them delegitimize Trump's influence in the country, so much so, that despite having a Republican majority, they are unable to pass bills. This shows just how far the far left Democratic Party will go to try and show how weak the presidency has truly become when even good events like the return of American civilians from North Korean prisons or the trade deal with Mexico and Canada barely get any attention due to the state of the news cycle.

The Democratic Party would have you believe that Trump's failure to hold Russia accountable for its meddling in the 2016 elections also leads to a weakened democracy. This ridiculous and false grandstanding is nothing short of sad; Trump has held Russia accountable. It is true though that a legitimate presidency in a democratic state can only be presented if the election was fair and just.

The first intrusion of Russia into the United States election was through the work of Putin and his officials. Their shady dealings and alleged meetings with the staff of the Trump campaign laid doubt into the election proceedings. Soon politicians and lobbyists in the United States were scared to even hold a meeting with Sergey Kislyak, who was essentially just doing his job as the ambassador of Russia. Even associating with the Russian officials was seen as suspicious, but this did not stop Donald Trump. He held a meeting with Sergey Kislyak and another Russian official just a day after firing James Comey. He also had multiple meetings with Vladimir Putin and continued to praise him in the media.

In 2016, the FBI also began to release warnings about 'bad actors' at the voter registration stations. Continued hacking by Russians led to nationwide alerts by the FBI. Although no tampering occurred, it was estimated that the information of 200,000 voters was stolen. This may have had two main effects on the election in 2016. The first was the Democratic conspiracy theory of the formation of a strategy to make Donald Trump win that was formed by the Russian Institute for Strategic Studies. The Democrats believed that they developed multiple ways in which they could change Clinton's win into a loss. This may have been a small part in the move to weaken the presidency and democracy.

The second effect was the wave of fake news and targeting trolls that swamped social media platforms. In Michigan alone, right before the election, more than half of the news on social media was false, According to the Democrats. This soon became a recurring theme everywhere and failure to control the issue may have led to some serious fake election interference news. Russian propaganda was allegedly rampant on platforms like Facebook and Twitter and it encompassed some of the most polarizing issues of the country like Obamacare, abortion, immigration, global warming, etc. A lot of advertisements and pages were linked to Russian troll farms that began to divide the voters further with rampant misinformation. Unfortunately, the Democratic Party made this a much bigger issue than it actually was. In fact, they found less than $50,000 in fake ads might have been put up. This is a very small amount when compared to the billions of dollars that the Hillary Clinton Campaign and the Democratic Party put into effect.

This would not have been a big issue if as a nation the politicians denounced such news. Instead, Trump and the Democratic Party used a lot of these sentiments to fuel voters on both sides. This was an endless cycle that worked in tandem as a catalyst to each other.

This is not the only way the Democrats felt Russia has used President Donald Trump to further their own agenda in terms of geopolitical issues. His strained relationship with some of the most prominent world leaders like German Chancellor, Angela Merkel, and French President, Emmanuel Macron are looked at by the Democrats as weakening the American democracy. That could not be further from the truth. Trumps aggressive and dominant personality has made these leaders more mindful of taking advantage of American generosity to the world.

Some say this can be seen in the way Donald Trump severed friendly relations through his trade policies that led to considerable outrage among leaders of the world. He made America stand alone on global warming as all the leaders of the world convened to save the planet. His stance on NATO also led to prominent figures in the politics shaking their heads at his actions. He even finished the Iran Deal against the advice of world leaders around the globe.

His acceptance of making change for the betterment of America and its citizens has drawn harsh criticism from the far left and Democratic critics. His worldview on making all allied countries pay up for broken promises to our country that other past presidents were too weak to enforce shows that America can stand alone. When needed, we can unite for the common good of our society and the world as a whole. We must always remember that with elected officials the few make the decisions for the many. The President needs to have diplomacy with even dictators to get them to do what he needs them to do. He also needs to be strong when being taken advantage of by our Allies, those whom we call our friends as well as take and take from us within the return. The weakening of our institutions is driven by those who care only for their personal agendas. The Democratic leaders have only been a constant obstruction for the country moving forward. There old faded leaders cry like Chuck Schumer and Nancy Pelosi has started to fall on deaf ears.

Setting this false story obsession by the far left and the Democratic Leadership, that Trump's illiteracy of America's institution weakens America's position in the international community. Historically, America has always benefitted greatly with its partnership with European countries. It lends the nation considerable soft power that benefits both mutually and promotes the ideals of peace, freedom, and democracy, but it also does not come without a price. A hefty price that America has paid for over many decades, to the point that enough is enough. Being our friend should not cost us billions of dollars and lost trade goods and jobs. Friends should not take advantage of their friends, which is what Trump stands for. Germany has the US as a defender of Russian aggression, but then and goes on to sign a billion dollar agreement to buy Russian fuel, and not buy ours. We have to pay for the military bases around the world; these Countries do not let us have them for free. Trump's agenda is a plain bold commonsense approach to managing our country's affairs.

His America-first approach should be embraced by all, but unfortunately, it is not. Trumps hard edge approach has been working to the point that we have just signed new trade agreements with Mexico and Canada, which is now more mutually beneficial and fair to the United States. The Democratic Leadership will also try and sell that Trump praises Vladimir Putin. This is an obsession of the Democrats, as a false one, but never the less an obsession. The Democratic Leadership didn't hate Putin when Obama was in Office. Now it is Trump's turn to carry the torch and fight Russian President Putin. This is always the fact when the weak run behind the strong for safety. Or it could be that the Democratic Leadership under Obama never had the guts to stand up for America and its values.

Recently, Antifa and other dissident groups have also grown in size to opposing Trump's government. They were essentially groups against racism, white supremacists, Neo-fascism, and Neo-Nazis, but have increasingly become anti-government as time passes. They think that the Trump era is turning towards authoritarian regimes, which is simply not true since this government follows the democratic process just like previous administrations. This view is why they strive to fight against every policy by Donald Trump.

They aim to disrupt far-right speakers and alt-right events and use a variety of tactics to do this. They are an extreme alt-left group that doesn't shy away from violence using bricks, knives, chains and pepper sprays. They justify their violence saying that it's just self-defense but this isn't true. They have actually been really successful in cutting short or canceling of speeches and rallies. They are an unlawful group that has focused their efforts on hindering actual positive action as well if it's coming from the right wing politicians and workers.

They were the main group that protested the 2016 election of Donald Trump. They put a damper on a democratic Process just because it wasn't to their particular liking. They fail to realize that Trump did win the election in through the Electoral College. This failure dampers them from seeing the fact that if Trump succeeds so will the United States.

It is not productive to America when the president has violent death threats from such violent groups. Recently, in September of 2018, some prominent members of the Trump presidency have also received dangerous Ricin powders in envelopes including Ted Cruz and James Mattis. Such attempts to weaken the presidency can only harm America as a whole.

# Chapter 5: In Conclusion

It is important to realize that Donald Trump will only be an effective president if the whole country works together to get behind the president. As citizens, it is surely important to hold their politicians accountable, but this does not mean that they begin to hinder the process of the government.

It is necessary for the public to view the news objectively and try to find different perspectives on the same issues. This will give them a more objective view so that they can see the issue from more than one side.

Such a perspective is much-needed on issues like politics. This is because it is important to look at a situation without the restricted lens of the party. This will help the presidency of America succeed on a national and international level. At the end of the day, isn't that what every American citizen wants?

It is also important to hold those people accountable who go out of their way to hurt the presidency. It is the right of every citizen to protest, but violent protestors with agendas like the Antifa and dissident groups need to be held accountable. They work to hinder the process of the government, rather than make America better. They put their personal views above the rest of the nation's wishes and interest.

The nation is only as powerful and successful as its leader. Since Donald Trump is the president, it is important to do everything we can as citizens to understand the mission and vision of his cabinet. This will only help to Make America Great Again.

www.ingramcontent.com/pod-product-compliance
Lightning Source LLC
Chambersburg PA
CBHW062121040426
42336CB00041B/2228